Until Christ is Formed

By Bishop Sandra Hayden

Until Christ is Formed
Copyright © 2011 by Bishop Hayden

All rights reserved. No part of this book may be reproduced or transmitted in any form or by any means without written permission from the author.

The Bible versions used in this book are the King James, New King James, New International Version and the Amplified Bible

ISBN: 978-0-615-64188-1

Cover Design by Donald Peart Jr.
Contact Info: DonPeart.com

Dedication

I have dedicated this book to my family, all my spiritual sons and daughters of the Apostolic Alliance. Special thanks to apostle Donald Peart, Prophetess Judith Peart, Crown of Glory Ministries, and Dr Anya Hall for provoking me to jealousy [zeal] unto this good work.

Table of Contents

A New Creation	*1*
A Child is Born	*5*
Jacob was Created, Israel was Formed	*9*
Put on Christ	*13*
The Seed Must Die	*19*
Metamorphosis	*27*
God is a Finisher	*35*
Author's Biographical Sketch	

Chapter 1
A New Creation

2 Corinthians 5:17a
... If anyone is in Christ, he is a new creation.

"I'm so glad that the Lord saved me" is the song we were singing when I was a young lady attending the Baptist church, not really knowing what it meant to be saved. One day a visiting minister came to our church and explained to me what it meant to be saved. I always loved attending services and singing on the choir, but something was missing because there was still a war going on in me, a struggle not to be influenced by my peers.

As I began to study the Word of God I received wisdom and revelation of what it means to be saved, but also to become a son of God. According to 2 Corinthians 5:17, if any man be in Christ, he is a new creature and new species of being with the DNA of our heavenly Father. Yet, there remain eternal struggles from within.

One day I opened my Bible to read the Word of God in Galatians 4:19. The Apostle Paul in his writing to the church in Galatia encouraged them not to go back into legalism. He also encouraged the Galatians to have a zeal for the true gospel of grace. He uses the affectionate phrase "my little children," being their spiritual father with great love and concern for their spiritual growth and development, expressing the need for the nature of Christ to be formed in them.

Galatians 4:19, AMP
*My little children, for whom I am again suffering birth pangs until Christ is completely and permanently **formed (molded) within you**.*

Paul understood something about internal warfare according to his writings in Romans 7:14-25. In his own effort, he did not find the way to do what is right. He found himself doing things he did not approve of *(Romans 7:16)*.

Romans 7:16-17
*[16] If, then, I do what I will not to do, I agree with the law that it is good. [17] But now, it is **no longer** I who do it, but sin that dwells in me.*

In Roman 7: 17, Eventually Paul realized that it was "no longer I who do it but sin that dwells in me." The Greek adverb "no longer" signifies an "absolute" action. Paul realized that it was absolutely not him who was sinning, but sin in his flesh. However, there is hope for all of us who have the same struggles.

Romans 6:16
*Knowing this, that our **old man was crucified with him**, that the **body of sin** might be done away with that we should no longer be slaves of sin.*

The "old" man is the believer's unregenerate self. The Greek word for "old" does not refer to something old in years but to something that is worn out and useless. Our old self died with Christ and the life we enjoy now is a new divinely-given life that is the life of Christ himself.

We have been removed from the "unregenerate self" presence and control. So we should not follow the remaining memories of its old sinful ways as if we were still under its evil influence.

Ephesians 4:22
*That ye **put off** concerning the former conversation the old man, which is corrupt according to the deceitful lusts;*

In Ephesians 4:22, "put off" means "to strip away", as in taking off old filthy clothes and "old man" means the worn out, useless and unconverted sinful nature corrupted by deceit. Ephesians 4:23 23 says to "be renewed in the spirit of your mind which is the center of thought, understanding and belief, as well as motives and action."

We become a new man by faith. And our mind has to be renewed from the "old" way of thinking. In the new birth, we are considered "new" not "old" through faith in Jesus Christ.

Romans 10:10, AMP
For with the heart a person believes (adheres to, trusts in, and relies on Christ) and so is justified (declared righteous,

acceptable to God), and with the mouth he confesses (declares openly and speaks out freely his faith) and confirms [his] salvation.

The new birth is just that, a birth. A baby has its whole life before him as he leans to explore the world about him. Upon our new birth experienced as believers we have not tasted the whole of our Christian experience.

We must go from conception to perfection (maturity). The new birth is the beginning of our salvation. We are to work out our salvation with fear and trembling. Philippians 2:12 tells us to "work out your own salvation". The Greek verb rendered "work out" means to continually work to bring something to fulfillment or completion. It refers to the believer's responsibility for active pursuit of obedience in the process of sanctification.

Chapter 2
A Child is Born

Isaiah 9:6
*For unto us **a child is born,** unto us a son is given.*

We are born into the kingdom as children of God. Paul taught this to the Church at Galatia. According to Galatians 4:1, Paul said "that the heir as long as he is a child, does not differ from a slave, though he is master of all."

The Greek word for "child" refers to a child too young to talk, a minor spiritually and intellectually immature, and not ready for the privileges and responsibilities of adulthood.

We are heirs of God and joint heirs with Christ **(Romans 8:17).** Christ who is heir of all things appointed by God the Father, every believer has received by divine grace the full inheritance Christ receives by divine right. Many believers do not know or understand their inheritance.

In Hosea 11:1 God said when Israel was a child He loved him. However, he (the nation of Israel) was a child without wisdom. God loves us as His children and the church is "the Israel of God." We must move beyond the childhood stage to full-grown maturity.

The Apostle Paul, in I Corinthians 13, said that when he was a child, **he talked** like a child, **he thought** like a child,

he reasoned like a child. He said he put away childish things (childish things are disobedience, strife, jealousy, envy, backbiting, and the list goes on and on).

Children are self-centered and selfish. They want what they want when they want it and when they can't have their way, they have a temper <u>tantrum</u>. This is what we see in the body of Christ; someone who has not matured, will not receive **discipline** nor **correction** so they move from church to church, never growing up in the things of the spirit, having a temper <u>tantrum</u>.

The Scripture says, "If you are not **disciplined** (and everyone undergoes discipline), then you are illegitimate children and not true sons" *(Hebrews 12:8, NIV)*. Hebrews 12:3 also tells us to consider him; Jesus is the supreme example of willingness to suffer in obedience to God. Hebrews 12:5 says "do not despise the chastening of the Lord nor be discouraged when you are rebuked by him."

Hebrews 12:6 says "For whom the Lord loves he chastens, and scourges every son whom he receives". Respect for God equals submission to his will and love. You must willingly receive the Lord's chastening to have a richer, more abundant life.

Many times the Lord has brought correction into my life through His word and those who were my spiritual parents, especially the late Archbishop Benson Idahosa. Today I'm grateful for correction and impartation from that great man of God.

Proverbs 2:1-2 says "My son, if you will receive my words and treasure my commands with you, so that you incline your ear to wisdom and apply your heart to understanding." You must take the word of God and make it your own by faith and obedience. Once wisdom is applied and properly valued, both ear and mind are captivated by it.

Chapter 3
Jacob was Created, Israel was Formed

Isaiah 43:1a
*..The LORD ... **created** you, O Jacob, And He who **formed** you, O Israel ....*

Jacob was created. God brought Jacob into existence through his sovereign grace. In addition "Israel" had to be "formed." Jacob was a "trickster," before God **"formed" him** into a prince that had power with God. God showed that "Israel" was now "formed" when God changed Jacob's name to Israel.

Genesis 32:28
*And he said, **Thy name shall be called no more Jacob**, but **Israel:** for as a prince hast thou **power** with God and with men, and hast prevailed.*

Isaiah 43:1
*But now, thus says the LORD, who **created** you, O Jacob, And He who **formed** you, O Israel: "Fear not, for I have redeemed you; I have called you by your name; You are Mine.*

The word "formed" in Hebrew is "yatsar" meaning, "to press, be narrow, squeezed into shape, to mold into a form especially as a potter." In Jeremiah 18, God said to Jeremiah "go to the potter's house." At the potter's house, the potter was making a vessel at the wheel, but the vessel was marred. Since the vessel was marred, the potter decided to "form" another vessel as it pleased him.

We are the clay, marred, in the hands of the Potter (God our Creator). It is in the mind of the Potter what the design is for the clay. God is He who forms the clay into its purpose. We have to be careful how we complain to our maker as He forms us into the image of Christ.

Shall the clay say to him who forms it, "what are you making?" You cannot contend with God on His plans for your life. Remember, the word "formed" also occurs in the sense of God's framing or devising something in his mind.

His preordained purpose

Isaiah 37:26 "Hast thou not heard long ago, how I have done it and of ancient times, that I have **formed** it now have I brought it to pass". One of the meanings of God creating the nation of Israel is the understanding that God brought Israel it into existence. However, God also had to "form" Israel into His preordained purpose. We were predetermined to be formed into Christ's image.

"For whom He foreknew, He also **predestined** [to be] **conformed** to the image of His Son" *(Romans 8:29)*. This forming of God's purpose into us is linked to our wilderness experience. The wilderness experience is a divine must. **It** is in our wilderness experience we are shaped and conformed to the image of Christ.

Luke 4:1-2
*¹Then Jesus, being filled with the Holy Spirit, returned from the Jordan and was **led by the Spirit into the wilderness** ²being tempted for forty days by the devil ….*

Jesus was led into the wilderness being tempted of the devil for forty days by the devil. Forty is the number of testing. Jesus was full of the spirit. He received the Spirit without measure. He was led. There was a great urgency by the Spirit. God has a company of "led" ones who will embrace their wilderness experience to be formed into Christ's image.

And the devil said to him

Satan is a liar and the Father of lies. There is no truth in him. The Devil questioned Jesus' sonship in the wilderness. "And the devil said to Him, "If You are the Son of God, command this stone to become bread." *(Luke 4:3)*.

"If you are the Son of God" should be translated as "**since** you are the Son of God, command … bread." He wanted Jesus to use his power for personal gratification, which was outside the will of God.

Part of the process of being formed into Christ's image is to be able to resist the frivolous use of power when the devil tempts us to abuse power. Whenever the devil attempts to speak to you, you must answer him with, "It is written." Jesus was established in the word of God; and the Word of God must also be established in your hearts.

Jesus was quoting the word, Deuteronomy 8:3: "He humbled you and suffered you to hunger and fed you with manna, which you knew not, neither did your fathers know what was in your heart whether you would keep his commandments". Again, the question is: in the test, how will you act? How will you react?

Luke 8:13, discusses the parable of the seed and the soil. Many come and hear the word (the seed) with joy. We say things like "that was the word", "that was revelation", "the word blessed me."

However, because there is no root; because there is no depth in them; they are shallow soil, or surface Christian; they believe for a while but in the time of testing, they stop praying, they stop reading the word, they blame God and sometimes they blame their leaders, not realizing it's only a test, the trying or testing of their faith.

I remember watching TV and the program would be interrupted and the voice would say, "This is only a test." Then the program would resume. James says in James 1:13 God cannot be tempted nor does he tempt us. We are tested in our faith for the purpose of our spiritual growth and development.

Chapter 4
Put on Christ

Galatians 3:27
For as many of you have been baptized into Christ have **put on Christ.**

Christ being formed in us is another way of saying we must "put on Christ." In order for us to put on Christ, we must realize that we also died with Christ. We have been baptized into Jesus' death at Calvary.

Galatians 2:20
I am crucified with Christ: nevertheless I live; yet not I, but Christ liveth in me ....

When Christ died on the cross, in the mind of God, we also died with Christ. He became our substitute. Our identification with Him in His death gives us all the benefits for which He died. He died for you and me, and every believer.

Colossians 3 teaches that when we put on the new man, we are actually putting on Christ. This new man is that new creation man of 2 Corinthians 5:16-17 that has nothing to do with the flesh nature.

We cannot make any provision for our flesh. We must "put off" or "mortify" the sinful members (practices) of our physical bodies. We must give the Holy Spirit latitude to work in our lives.

According to Colossians 3:7-8, in the past (before we confessed Christ as savior and Lord) we walked in some things (anger, filthy speaking, etc) that we should get rid of. We must allow Christ to be formed in us. One of the primary ways of Christ being formed in us is to make Jesus Lord and not just Savior. Many want Jesus to be savior but not Lord.

When we say Christ is our Lord, it means he is master of our lives. The word "Lord" means "master, owner". We are not our own. We have been bought with a price, the Blood of Jesus. Therefore, allow Jesus to form His image **"in"** us.

It says in I Corinthians 3:16 we are the temple where the Spirit of God abides. Our physical bodies must be a living sacrifice. If we fail to function in God's prescribed order, it opens the believer up to Satan, which will ultimately result in distraction.

For the temple of God is Holy, which temple we are. By virtue of being in Christ and Christ in us, we are holy. We remain holy by the work of the Holy Spirit. Let Him work to form Christ in us.

In Ephesians 4:22 where it says "put off concerning the former conversation (the former manner of life)" <u>the old man</u> refers to the unsaved person dominated by the totally depraved nature. The rest of the verse says "which is corrupt according to the deceitful lusts."

The unsaved person is subject to a continuous process of corruption. Paul continued in Ephesians 4:23 by saying, "And be renewed (a continuous act) in the spirit of your mind." As believers, we must be pulled from dependence on self to a total dependence on Christ by renewing our minds.

Paul continued in Ephesians 4: 24 saying, "put on the new man." We are a new man by virtue of being baptized into his death, buried with him by baptism into death. We must put on this new man.
That is, allow the Christ nature to be formed in us. Therefore put away lying or falsehood *(Ephesians 4:25)*. Lying also includes exaggerations, fabrications, cheating, making false promises, betraying a confidence. making false excuses are all forms of lying.

We must remember the letter of Ephesians was written to the church, not the world. It is time to return to the Bible and the glorious gospel of the Kingdom of God. In Paul's writings to the church at Corinth, in 1 Corinthians 3, he addresses their carnal state.

He could not address them as mature believers, but as babes in Christ. (This word was given to people who considered themselves to be spiritual giants yet not fully controlled by the Holy Spirit.) Paul said they were "carnal," controlled by the fallen flesh.

Romans 7:14
*For we know that **the law is spiritual**, but I am **carnal**, sold under sin.*

The law is spiritual which reflects God's holy character. The spiritual law is totally of God and from God. Paul then contrasted human's "carnality" as opposed to the spiritual law. Paul was saying the law is not bad.

It is humans' "carnal" nature that has to be changed from "carnality." "Carnal" means "fleshly." Thus, Christ's spiritual nature has to be formed in us, as we put off the carnal nature—the body of death, or the sins of the flesh.

It is only through Christ and faith in His finished work that we are delivered from the body of death. The Church has to move from carnality to spiritual in order to receive the deeper things of Jesus. The Apostle says to the Corinthian believers he fed them with milk, the more easily digestible truths of doctrine that are given to new believers.

Solid food is the deeper features of the doctrine of Scriptures. The difference is not in the kind of truth, but degree of depth in the Spirit of God. Spiritual immaturity makes one unable to receive the richest truths.

When believers are walking in envy and strife, they are "carnal." Because carnality produces the attribute of envy, a severe form of selfishness which produces the action of strife and the subsequent divisions. We have witnessed church splits, members running from church to church, tearing down leaders and ministries because of envy and strife.

The Bible says where there is envy and strife there is confusion and every evil work. This is one of the reasons we have not been effective in making a difference in the world because of the evil workings of envy and strife. They are body killers. The Church must change this attitude and allow the Christ nature to be formed in them

There is no need for jealousy in the body for each member has been called to their God-given assignments, each operating in their individual gifting and anointing. You need to seek God for your assignment. Be who God "formed" you to be. Flow in your gifting and anointing.

God has placed all the gifts of the body as it has pleased him *(1 Corinthians 12:28).* The diversities of gifts are given by the Holy Spirit. They are sovereignty and supernaturally bestowed to help "form" us into the image of Christ *(Ephesians 4:11-13).*

We are not allowed to place ourselves into certain offices. We are not allowed to form ourselves into our own images. This is one of the reasons we see self-appointed bishops, prophets and apostles, men trying to function in an office not formed, ordained or sanctioned by God, trying to operate in the spirit realm where they do not qualify or have the authority. Little children let Christ be formed in you to mold your vessel into His purpose.

Chapter 5
The Seed Must Die

John 12:24
*Most assuredly, I say to you, unless a grain of wheat falls into the ground and **dies**, it remains alone; but if it dies, it produces much grain.*

Christ being formed in us is also linked to the death (crucifixion) of Jesus. In the book of Isaiah Chapter 53, the Holy Spirit speaks to us of the sufferings of our Lord Jesus. Isaiah 53:10 says it pleased God to bruise Him (this refers to the sufferings of Christ, which proceeded from the determinate counsel and foreknowledge of God). The Father saw with satisfaction the Son's self-sacrifice; as He witnessed with joy man's Redemption.

"**He [God] has put him to grief**" or He has put him to "sickness." This spoke of the time Jesus was on the cross, when God would make Jesus' soul an "**offering**" for all sins. The word "offering" in the Hebrew is "Asham" and means "a trespass offering", an "offering for sin". Christ was both the sin offering and the guilt offering.

The life of Christ was the Seed offering planted in the earth that God the Father would reap a harvest of other sons. Hebrews 2:10 says "For it became him whom are all things and by whom are all things in **bringing many sons to glory.**" This speaks of the divine purpose to make Jesus, the

"Captain of their salvation perfect through sufferings." Christ had to suffer on a cross in order to bring about redemption for humanity.

"Jesus was the firstborn among many sons" ***(Romans 8:29).*** When a seed is placed in the rich dark soil, there is the pressure of the gardener making sure that no air or light can possibly reach the seed. Death is imminent for the seed. As the days pass, the seed shell begins to wither.

John 12:24 says "verily, verily I say unto you, except a corn of wheat fall into the ground and die, it abideth alone, but if (in the event that it does) it brings forth much fruit." The sown kernel dies to bring forth a rich harvest. In this parable, Jesus was speaking of his death.

When we choose to follow Jesus to be conformed to His image, we must also embrace the law of death. We must die to our will, in order to be conformed to God's will. Jesus didn't come to do his will (his own thing) but the will of his Father. There are no short cuts in the Kingdom of God; too many want to avoid the making process of God.

Deliverance will not come only through the laying on of hands, but also by dying to the flesh. People come to Church wanting hands laid on them without doing the necessary work for deliverance. I can pray for you to have patience, but the Bible says tribulation works patience ***(Romans 5:3).*** Patience requires "time" to work through the difficulties we face.

In order for us to know the life us Christ, and be conformed to the "resurrection life" of Christ; we must be willing to die to our carnal nature. Dead men don't lie; they aren't jealous, envious, competitive or vindictive.

Jesus said in John 12:25, "If you love your life (or soul) you will lose it, and he who hates his life (or soul) in this world will keep it for eternal life." Jesus is saying, loving your "self-life" will not allow you to see fulfillment in life. We must hate our "self-life," make our desires last; and make Christ's desires first in all things.

John 15:1
I am the true vine, and My Father is the vinedresser.

Christ is the true vine. The vine is the pathway for nutrients getting to the branches. Jesus alone is the source of life; and His Father (our Father also) is the Vinedresser. God is the Vinedresser; and He is the owner of the garden.

Song of Solomon 4:12 says "A garden enclosed is my sister, my spouse; a spring shut up, a fountain sealed." The word "sister" is a common ancient near-Eastern term of endearment by a husband for his wife, which expresses classiness and permanence of relationship.

We the bride, the garden of God have allowed ourselves to be closed, not giving the Spirit of God total access to our lives.

A Spring Shut up

Jesus spoke in John 7:38, indicating that if we believe on him that which has been accomplished at Calvary, out of our belly (innermost being) shall flow rivers of living water. This living water is the Holy Spirit. As the river of the Spirit overflows in your life it brings life to others.

Ezekiel 47:9, KJV says "And it shall come to pass, that everything that liveth, which moveth, whithersoever the rivers shall come, shall live: and there shall be a very great multitude of fish, because these waters shall come thither: for they shall be healed; and everything shall live whither the river cometh." This is a prophetic word of that which is to come, but it is also a "now-word" (present application) to believers.

As the river flows (the Holy Spirit) in your life, as a witness of the saving grace of Christ, great multitude of fish (many souls, because we are called to be fishers of men) will come into the kingdom of God.

No longer I that Live

Galatians 2:20
I have been crucified with Christ; ***it is no longer I who live****, but Christ lives in me; and the life which I now live in the flesh I live by faith in the Son of God, who loved me and gave Himself for me.*

Embracing the "law of identification" doesn't mean God annihilates that person. The "law of identification" is more internal. Paul stated that he had been crucified with Christ; and it was no longer (Paul) or you or I who is living; but it is Christ who now lives **"in"** me, and you, and the life which we now live in the flesh, we live by faith in the Son of God, who loved me and delivered Himself up for me.

We must live the life of Christ in a fleshly body. Our bodies are houses for Christ to live in. As we yield to the law of identification, Christ lives his life through us. Paul recognized that He lived the life of Christ not by his own strength or ability. Our daily walk before God, as we now live in flesh, must be lived by faith of the Son of God. The finished work of the cross is the object of our faith. We must be conformed to Jesus' death, burial and resurrection.

Without the Divine Seed (Christ) in us, we will never be able to live the Christ life. Romans 12:1 speak to us of our consecration as Paul writes to the church in Rome. Paul begged the Christians at Rome to "present their bodies a living sacrifice" Only you can present you, not your Pastor or your Apostle.

In other words, it's your personal responsibility. It is with grateful obedience that we respond to God's request by offering ourselves to God. Because of the grace of God, salvation flows from God's mercy. Mercy frees us from the misery that accompanies the consequences of sin.

Through Jesus sacrifice and resurrection, God only accepts "living sacrifices" under the New Covenant. Under the old covenant, God accepted the sacrifice of dead animals. But because of Christ's ultimate sacrifice the Old Testament "dead" sacrifices are no longer of any effect *(Hebrews 9:11-12)*.

We must yield our bodies as an instrument of righteousness. Romans 6:12-13 says "Therefore do no let sin reign in your mortal (death doomed) body that you should obey it in its lust, and do not **present** your members as instruments of unrighteousness to sin, but present yourselves to God as being alive from the dead and your members as instruments of righteousness to God."

"Present" here in verse 13 refers to a decision of the will. Before sin can have power over a believer, it must first pass through that person's will. Instruments of unrighteousness are tools for accomplishing that which violates God holy law and will.

Romans 12:1
I beseech you therefore, brethren, by the mercies of God, that you present your bodies **a living sacrifice***, holy, acceptable to God, which is your* **reasonable** *service.*

Paul also stated that presenting ourselves as a living sacrifice is our "reasonable service." "Reasonable service" is also translated as our "spiritual act of worship." Reasonable is from the Greek for "logical."

It is logical to God and should be logical to us to offer ourselves to God because of what Jesus did for us. We owe God our highest form of service; because of what He has done for us through His grace, mercy and the finished work of Christ.

Chapter 6
Metamorphosis

Romans 12:2
*And do not be **conformed** to this world, but be **transformed** by the renewing of your mind, that you may prove what is that good and acceptable and perfect will of God.*

Do not be conformed to this world. This word "conformed" refers to assuming an outward expression that does not reflect what is really inside, a kind of masquerade or act. We are not to be conformed to this world (age) or conformed to the beliefs of this world's system, or conformed to the world's values, or the spirit of the age.

We believers are to be "transformed" to Christ image. This is the Greek word from which the English word "metamorphosis" comes from. "Metamorphosis" means a change in inward and outward appearance. "Metamorphosis" is also used to describe our transformation ("change") into Christ image from glory to glory in 2 Corinthians. This is the same word used to describe Christ's transfiguration.

Matthew 17:2
*And was **transfigured** before them: and his face did shine as the sun, and his raiment was white as the light.*

Christ, in His "metamorphosis," briefly displayed outwardly His "inner" divine nature and His glory at the transfiguration. We must outwardly manifest our inner, redeemed nature on a daily basis.

Renewing of your mind

Romans 12:2
*And do not be conformed to this world, but be transformed by **the renewing of your mind, that** you may prove what is that good and acceptable and perfect will of God.*

This transformation will only occur as we allow the Holy Spirit to change our thinking or renovate our minds through study and meditation of God's word. Psalm 119:11 says "Your word have I laid up in my heart, that I might not sin against thee." Your heart must be home to the scripture before your lips can declare the word. Psalm 119:12 says "Blessed are You, O Lord; teach me Your statutes".

The Holy Spirit is the Teacher. He will give revelation and illumination to the Word as you study, not just reading the Word of God. Revelation knowledge comes also from the ministry gifts given to the body of Christ: the apostles, prophets, evangelists, pastors, and teachers.

How much time do you spend in the Word compared to your time watching movies, playing video games or other entertainment? We tend to find or make time for whatever we want to do. However, we must once again make God's

Word our top priority for mind renewal. A renewed mind is one that is saturated with the Word of God and is controlled by the Word of God.

Good, acceptable, and perfect will

Romans 12:2
*And do not be conformed to this world, but be transformed by the renewing of your mind, that you may prove what is that **good and acceptable and perfect will of God.***

Paul also indicated that we are to prove the "good", "acceptable" and "perfect" will of God by renewing our minds. Holy living is what God approves. We don't hear teachings anymore on holy living, which is to be the lifestyle of the believer. We live in a time that men are doing what seems right in their own eyes.

2 Peter 2:14-15
*[14] having **eyes** full of adultery and that cannot cease from sin, enticing unstable souls. They have a heart trained in covetous practices, and are accursed children. [15]They have forsaken the right way and gone astray, following the way of Balaam the son of Beor, who loved the wages of unrighteousness.*

In Romans 12:2, quoted above, the words "good", "acceptable" and "perfect" are borrowed from Old Testament sacrificial language and describe a life that is morally and spiritually spotless, as the sacrificial animals were to be.

Leviticus 22:18-19
*¹⁸"Speak to Aaron and his sons, and to all the children of Israel, and say to them: 'Whatever man of the house of Israel, or of the strangers in Israel, who offers his sacrifice for any of his vows or for any of his freewill offerings, which they offer to the LORD as a burnt offering—¹⁹you shall offer of your own free will a male **without blemish** from the cattle, from the sheep, or from the goats.*

The sacrifices could not have any spot nor blemish to be acceptable to the Lord. It could not be polluted. We are without fault through Jesus Christ as we offer our bodies according to His "**good and acceptable and perfect will.**"

Pressing toward the mark

Philippians 3:13-14
¹³ Brethren, I do not count myself to have apprehended ... ¹⁴ I press toward the goal for the prize of the upward call of God in Christ Jesus.

Paul said he had not attained or was not already perfect. In the Scriptures, Paul also uses the analogy of a runner to describe the Christian spiritual growth. Our goal is to be like Christ, to be conformed into his very image—character.

Like a runner in a race, we must continue to pursue Christ Goal for our lives to be conformed to His image. Paul said he pressed on. The Greek word was used of a sprinter and refers to aggressive, energetic chase.

1 Corinthians 9:24-27
*^{24}Do you not know that those who **run** in a race all run, but one receives the prize? **Run** in such a way that you may obtain it. ^{25}And everyone who competes for the prize is temperate in all things. Now they do it to obtain a perishable crown, but we for an imperishable crown. ^{26}Therefore **I run** thus: not with uncertainty. Thus I fight: not as one who beats the air. ^{27}But I discipline my body and bring it into subjection, lest, when I have preached to others, I myself should become disqualified.*

Paul pursued sanctification with all his might, straining every spiritual muscle to win the prize Paul wanted to "lay hold" of that for which Christ Jesus has also laid hold of him. "Lay hold" means to make one's own possession.

Paul had to forget his past works in order to continue to chase the prize of the upward calling of being conformed to the image of Christ. Paul had to forget those things (old works, pedigree, etc) which were behind him. We cannot rely on our past deeds and achievements even in ministry or dwell on sins and failure of our past.

We must always be reaching forward! Yet the question must be asked, what are you reaching forward to? For some, they are reaching for bigger platform, to travel in certain Christian circles, for some they are reaching for a great ministry.

There's nothing wrong with having a large ministry, being on television if that is what God has called you to do. But our highest goal is to be Christ-like here and now. We are to be walking in maturity and sonship.

In Philippians 3:15, Paul says therefore let us (the body of Christ) as many as are mature (full grown) no longer babes tossed to and fro with every wind of doctrine, be likeminded in the pursuit of Christ-likeness. We must maintain the attitude of pursuing the prize of Christ-likeness.

Paul also stated that if we think otherwise to becoming like Jesus, God will "reveal" even this to you. Those who continue to dwell on the past and make no progress toward the goal of becoming like Jesus, God will reveal to them that they should be pursuing to be like Jesus Christ. The Greek word for "reveal" means: "to uncover or unveil".

We have seen and heard of God uncovering or unveiling many hidden things; because men refuse to press toward the goal of Christ likeness, by crucifying the deeds of their flesh. Paul then indicated that he was an example to follow. Paul also said to the degree that he have already "attained let us **walk** by the same rule."

The Greek word for "walk" refers to walking in line to stay in line spiritually and keep progressing in sanctification by the principles that had brought them to this point in their spiritual growth. In 1 Peter 2:1-2, Peter tells us to lay aside all malice, all deceit, hypocrisy, envy and all evil speaking. Why? Our new life can't grow unless sins are renounced. The Greek word for "evil" is used multiple times in the New Testament to indicate wickedness which comes from within a person.

Ephesians 4:31-32
[31] Let all bitterness, wrath, anger, clamor, and evil speaking be put away from you, with all malice. [32] And be kind to one another, tenderhearted, forgiving one another, just as God in Christ forgave you.

The verses above summarize some of the changes that are to take place in the life of a believer. Bitterness reflects a smoldering resentment; wrath has to do with uncontrolled rage, uncontrolled passion of a moment. Anger is a more internal, deep displeasure and hostility. Clamor is the outcry of strife out of control. Evil speaking is slander. Malice is the general Greek term for evil, the root of all vices. These are some of the practices we must change from.

We must change to become "kind to one another, tenderhearted, forgiving one another, just as God in Christ forgave you." We must desire the pure and sincere milk of the word. A newborn baby can only grow as he drinks his/her milk every three to four hours, crying, craving for his/her bottle of milk. Our spiritual growth is marked by our internal craving and delight in the Word of God.

Chapter 7
God is a Finisher

Galatians 5:19
*My little children, of whom I travail in birth again until Christ be **formed in you**,*

Philippians 1:6
*Being confident of this very thing, that He who has begun a good work in you will **complete it** until the day of Jesus Christ.*

We know that our heavenly Father is the Alpha and the Omega. Jesus said he finished the work or the assignment given to him. We must be confident that he (Christ) shall finish that good work which has begun in our lives. God will not stop until He 'forms" Christ in us.

According to Philippians 1:6, Jesus will complete His good work He has begun in us, the work of transforming us into His image and likeness. The Greek verb translated "has begun" used only here and in Galatians 3:3 is referencing the good work of salvation itself.

When God begins a work of salvation in a person, He finishes and perfects that work. This word "confident" means persuaded and points to the fact that the good work God began in you **will be** completed by God. This good work began before God formed you in your mother's womb.

Ephesians 1:1-4
*¹Paul, an apostle of Jesus Christ by the will of God, to the saints which are at Ephesus, and to the faithful in Christ Jesus: ² Grace be to you, and peace, from God our Father, and from the Lord Jesus Christ. ³Blessed be the God and Father of our Lord Jesus Christ, who hath blessed us with all spiritual blessings in heavenly places in Christ: {places: or, things} ⁴According as he hath chosen us in him **before the foundation of the world**, that we should be holy and without blame before him in love.*

Before God formed you, he knew you. In Jeremiah 1:5, God said to the prophet "before I formed you, I knew you and called you to be a prophet". We have been called "to be." What are you becoming?

Psalm 139:13-17
*¹³For thou hast possessed my reins: **thou hast covered me in my mother's womb.** ¹⁴I will praise thee; for I am fearfully and wonderfully made: marvellous are thy works; and that my soul knoweth right well. ¹⁵My substance was not hid from thee, when I was made in secret, and curiously wrought in the lowest parts of the earth. ¹⁶Thine eyes did see my substance, yet being unperfect; and **in thy book all my members were written,** which in continuance were fashioned, when as yet there was none of them. ¹⁷ How*

precious also are thy thoughts unto me, O God! how great is the sum of them!

According to David writing above, God spoke to you about His plan for your life before any of your bones began to grow in the womb of your mother. All of your members were written in Gods book prior to us being formed. In fact, we were "in God" before we were formed in our mother's womb.

In Paul's writing to the Ephesians believers and all believers, Paul showed them and us that God chose us **"in"** Him before the foundation of the world. The word **"in"** is the primary preposition and denotes fixed position, in place, time or state. God chose us for Himself and by Himself for the praise of his glory, **"in"** Himself!

We were chosen to be holy and without blame before Him. This describes both a purpose and a result of God's choosing those who are to be saved. We have been given Christ's imputed righteousness. We have been predestined into God's adoption as sons through the righteousness of Jesus.

Ephesians 1:4-5
*⁴According as he hath chosen us **in** him before the foundation of the world, that we should be holy and without blame before him in love: ⁵Having **predestinated** us unto the adoption of children by Jesus Christ to himself, according to the good pleasure of his will.*

"Predestination" means God determines what will happen. He sees, He knows, He plans, He prepares, He appoints and He decide what will happen. Isaiah 14:24 states that The LORD of hosts hath sworn, saying, Surely as I have thought, so shall it come to pass; and **as I have purposed, so shall it stand**"

We were also predestined to be adopted as sons. When we adopt a child we can bestow our love, resources and inheritance, but not our own distinct characteristics. Yet, God miraculously gives his own nature to those whom He has elected and who have trusted in Christ.

He makes us His children in the image of His divine Son giving us not just Christ's riches and blessings, but also Christ's very nature (Spirit). "For you did not receive the spirit of bondage again to fear, but you received the spirit of adoption by whom we cry out "Abba Father" *(Romans 8:15)*. May we travail in birth again until Christ be formed in us *(Galatians 4:19)*.

Author's Biographical Sketch:

Dr Sandra Hayden has a unique ministry demonstrated through the manifestation of healing, salvations of souls, miracles and the abundance of financial prosperity throughout her 35 years in ministry. In a generation where many leaders have "fallen away" from the mainstream ministry of Christ, Jesus, Dr Hayden remains consistent in her character and her integrity.

Dr. Sandra Hayden received her Doctorate in Theology from Oral Robert University, through the guidance of Bishop Benson Idahosa of Africa. Dr Hayden has ministered the Word of God with grace and style throughout North America, Scotland, Australia, Africa, and the Caribbean

Dr. Hayden is founder of the Apostolic Alliance a fellowship committed to addressing the needs of senior leaders and the fivefold ministry gifts. She is also the founder of "Loving Me, Loving You;" an one day women's conference established to uplift, encourage and empower a generation of women of all ages. Dr. Hayden founded Restoring Life Worship Center in Charlotte, NC; and New Community Development Corporation in Baltimore, MD.

Bishop Hayden also co-founded Word Alive Family Worship Center of which she was chief overseer in Baltimore, MD for over 19 years. Word Alive is now known as Kingdom Life Church under the leadership of her son, Pastor Michael Philip. This has freed her to go to the nations as an apostle.

Dr Hayden is a true apostolic gift to this generation. She has been ordained by God as a magnetic force that pulls people into the very presence of God, encouraging them to fulfill their destiny in Christ Jesus.

Contact Information:
Dr. Sandra Hayden Ministries
P.O. Box 11354
Baltimore, MD 21239
Email: Bishopatwork@aol.com

Notes

Notes

www.ingramcontent.com/pod-product-compliance
Lightning Source LLC
Chambersburg PA
CBHW051712090426
42736CB00013B/2659